Fitness

Perspectives on Physical Health

by Bonnie Graves

Consultant:
Charles T. Kuntzleman
Director, Fitness for Youth
University of Michigan

LifeMatters
an imprint of Capstone Press
Mankato, Minnesota

LifeMatters Books are published by Capstone Press
PO Box 669 • 151 Good Counsel Drive • Mankato, Minnesota 56002
http://www.capstone-press.com

Printed in the United States of America

Library of Congress Cataloging-in-Publication Data
Graves, Bonnie B.
     Fitness / by Bonnie Graves.
          p.   cm.—(Perspectives on physical health)
     Includes bibliographical references and index.
     Summary: Defines fitness and suggests different techniques and motivations that readers can use to improve their own level of fitness.
     ISBN 0-7368-0418-8 (book)—ISBN 0-7368-0438-2 (series)
     1. Physical fitness—Juvenile literature. [1. Physical fitness.] I. Title. II. Series.
     RA777 .G673 2000
     613.7—dc21

                                           99-054593
                                       CIP

Staff Credits
Rebecca Aldridge, editor; Adam Lazar, designer; Jodi Theisen, photo researcher

Photo Credits
Cover: The Stock Market/©Michael K. Daly
FPG International/©Rob Gage, 8; ©Bill Losh, 11; ©Jill Sabella, 17; ©Mark Harmel, 23; ©Michael Keller, 55
International Stock/©Joe Willis, 7, 59; ©Sunstar, 20; ©Arthur Holeman, 31; ©Bill Stanton, 52; ©Don Romero, 56
Photo Network/©David N. Davis, 41; ©M. Messenger, 49
Unicorn Stock Photos/©Martin R. Jones, 34; ©Paul Murphy, 37; ©Martin Jones, 38; ©Dick Young, 44
Uniphoto/©C. Yarbrough, 14; ©Llewellyn, 26; ©Lewis Portnov, 28; ©James Kay, 47
Visuals Unlimited/©L.S. Stepanowicz, 52; ©Cheyenne Rouse, 52

A 0 9 8 7 6 5 4 3 2 1

Table of Contents

Chapter Overview

Fitness is an essential part of being healthy.

Exercise is the means to fitness. It benefits every part of the body.

Exercise helps promote a fit heart, a trim body, a sound mind, a winning attitude, and a long life.

There are many ways teens can get and stay fit.

Chapter 1

Fitness—What's in It for You?

Track practice was over. Lisa
ran toward the parking lot where

LISA, AGE 16

Ty waited. He sat behind the wheel of his sports car. As Lisa
ran, she noticed a new ease in her stride. She felt her leg
muscles working. She took deep, even breaths of the spring
air. A couple of months ago, running was hard work for Lisa.
That was before she joined the track team. Now, Lisa loved
running and the energy it gave her. Lisa stopped a few feet
from Ty's car and grinned. "Want to race?"

A person does not have to play a sport or be a marathon runner to be fit. Any activity that gets a person moving around is better than none at all. Walking, riding a bike, and skating all help improve fitness. Vacuuming, raking the yard, taking the stairs instead of the elevator, and cleaning the garage increase activity.

Lisa experienced an improvement in her physical fitness. For her, it was just one reward of joining the track team.

What Is Fitness?

Physical fitness can be defined in many ways. A fit body is in good physical shape. It runs smoothly. Physical fitness means that a person's heart, lungs, muscles, and blood vessels are in good working order. The result is the ability to work and play with pleasure and energy. Fitness is important for today and for the future. It is an essential part of a healthy life.

Exercise Is Wise

Body, mind, and spirit all benefit from exercise. Regular exercise leads to a fit body. All body parts benefit from the right kind of exercise. Muscles, organs, bones, and ligaments, or the tough tissues that connect bones and hold some organs in place, all benefit. Exercise also benefits the brain and the nervous and digestive systems. Moderate exercise also can help boost the immune system. This means exercise may help ward off minor infections such as colds. Exercise improves emotional health, too.

A Strong Heart

The heart is at the core of fitness. It is the strongest muscle in the human body, and exercise makes it stronger. The heart gets its best workout through aerobic exercise. This type of exercise demands oxygen, but it should not leave a person gasping for breath. Aerobic exercises are repeated again and again to allow the muscles to get fresh oxygen over and over.

Repeated exercise of the heart muscle makes it stronger and larger. A fit heart beats slower than an unfit heart. That is because it pumps more blood with each beat. A healthy heart is prepared for stress. It won't wear out when the going gets tough.

Exercising the heart may increase the level of good cholesterol, or high-density lipoprotein (HDL). This fatty substance helps form certain hormones, or chemicals that control body functions. Cholesterol is needed to make cell membranes, or linings, and to help the nervous system function. This system controls all the actions of the body. High levels of good cholesterol have been linked to a lower risk of coronary artery disease. This disease affects the blood vessels, or passageways, to the heart.

A Trim Body

Exercise helps to keep your body weight right for your height. The food you eat contains energy that is measured in calories. The body burns the calories provided by the food you eat. However, if your body can't use all the calories, it stores the excess calories as fat. Exercise can burn the extra calories. The body uses them as fuel to keep going during physical activities.

A Sound Mind

Exercise helps the brain. It improves mental alertness. Studies show that students who regularly exercise perform better in school. Regular exercise helps in getting a better night's sleep, which also helps mental alertness. Exercise reduces stress and controls depression as well. Exercising causes the body to produce endorphins. These chemicals give people increased feelings of well-being.

A Winning Attitude

Another benefit of exercise is that it can boost self-esteem. People who exercise usually feel better about themselves. A program of regular exercise gives a sense of control. People who achieve their fitness goals often feel a sense of accomplishment.

Benefits of exercise:

More energy

Less stress

Better self-image

Increased resistance to fatigue

More relaxation and less tension

Better sleep

Toned muscles

Less body fat

Will's alarm rang at 5:30 A.M. Will groaned. Then he rolled out of bed and put on his workout clothes. Will's dad waited downstairs. After his dad's heart attack, Will and his dad made an agreement. They decided that three days a week they'd get up early and head for the gym. Neither of them had worked out much before the heart attack. But the doctor had made it clear—working out could combat the heart disease that ran in their family.

WILL, AGE 17

After leaving the gym, they went out for breakfast. Then Will's dad dropped Will off at school. Will kind of liked the whole experience. He enjoyed the dark, quiet mornings and the time alone with his dad. In fact, he looked forward to these times. They meant his dad would be around to share the ritual far into the future.

A Long, Happy Future

Physical fitness provides long-term as well as short-term benefits. Maintaining fitness over a lifetime generally means a longer life. A fit body reduces the risk of developing or dying from some of the leading causes of disease and illness. For example, regular physical activity reduces the risk of developing high blood pressure. It reduces the risk of developing diabetes, a disease in which there is too much sugar in the blood.

According to a 1996 report from the U.S. surgeon general, only about 50 percent of American youths regularly engage in physical activity. Twenty-five percent of American youths take part in no physical activity at all.

Researchers have shown that exercise can prevent some types of cancer. Females may help themselves by exercising during their teen and young adult years. Some research has shown exercise to reduce the chance of getting breast cancer and cancers of the reproductive system. However, further research needs to be done. Exercise also helps reduce the risk of colon cancer. The colon is a part of the large intestine. It increases the rate at which the body rids itself of waste. Colon cancer is a leading cause of cancer deaths among people in the United States.

Fitness and Teens

Some teens are very active. Some play and train for sports year-round. Others may balance a fitness program or a sport with other activities. Some teens exercise very little. Overall, about 50 percent of high school boys say they exercise enough to sweat and raise their heart rate. About 25 percent of girls say the same thing.

Teens don't exercise for many reasons. Many teens may not be aware of how important exercise is. Some teens may prefer to hang out with their friends or family. Others may enjoy more sedentary activities, or activities that require a lot of sitting. Such activities include listening to music, playing video games, and watching television.

Some schools and communities do not have enough funding for sports programs. Maintaining fitness in this way can cost a lot of money. Families may need to pay for program fees, uniforms, shoes, and protective gear. Some families cannot afford these things.

Fortunately, there are plenty of easy and inexpensive ways to get and stay fit. Many school- and community-supported sports are available. Teens can take physical eduation classes at school. They can participate in all sorts of outdoor and indoor fitness activities. To become fit, all that's needed is a little time and a lot of enthusiasm.

Points to Consider

What does being physically fit mean to you?

Do you think you are physically fit? Why or why not?

Do you think most people are physically fit? Why or why not?

Which of the benefits of fitness are the most important to you? Why?

How does fitness benefit a person in the long run?

Chapter Overview

Understanding the obstacles to fitness can help you overcome them.

Internal obstacles are things people do or think that keep them from achieving their goals. Some common internal obstacles are lack of motivation and time.

External obstacles may include the people and the world around someone. These obstacles prevent the person from achieving his or her goal. Common external obstacles to fitness are a person's family, friends, and community.

Both internal and external obstacles can be overcome through careful planning.

Chapter 2

The Challenges of Becoming Fit

"Can you believe Lidia?" Nita asked Beth. "I mean, she's really changed. She's so happy and full of energy. Besides, she looks great!"

"I know," Beth said. "I think it's basketball and all the exercise she's gotten since she joined the team."

"That convinces me. Tonight I start exercising! I'll ride my dad's stationary bike every day," Nita said.

That night Nita hopped on her dad's exercise bike. She started out enthusiastically. After a couple of days, she found the bike difficult and boring. After four days, she quit.

Knocking Down Road Blocks

Nita wanted to become fit. Often, however, desire is not enough. Frequently, there are obstacles to achieving fitness. Some of these obstacles, such as lack of motivation, are internal. They come from inside a person. Sometimes the obstacles come from the outside. These are external obstacles, such as not having money for good running shoes. Self-evaluation and planning can help a person overcome, or get over, many of these obstacles.

Realizing the Benefits

One internal obstacle to physical fitness is not realizing its benefits. Nita had overcome this obstacle. She understood that fitness is important in every teen's life. Fitness is something to be enjoyed by everyone—not just athletes like Lidia. Athletes may work out five or six times a week. In doing so, they become faster, stronger, and better at their sport. However, fitness still can be achieved at a more moderate rate. Three to four sessions a week also can keep a person physically fit.

Keeping Motivated

Unfortunately, Nita ran into another roadblock to fitness—lack of motivation. This is a common internal obstacle. Motivation means having the desire to do something. Getting fit takes effort. It requires more energy than reading or surfing the Internet. Sometimes it is hard to find the energy to do something strenuous.

Teens on sports teams may find motivation through competition. The desire to win keeps them practicing and working hard. Other teens may be motivated by a desire to improve their self-esteem or their mood. Some teens may want more muscle or a sleeker body. Others may just want fun.

Making Time

Many people feel that they do not have enough time to exercise. Lack of time is a common obstacle. It's true that fitness takes time to achieve and maintain. Experts suggest that people plan workouts into their weekly schedule. Many people think they will exercise in their free time. However, they usually end up putting off a workout to do other things.

Many members of sports teams know the importance of putting in time. Teams practice and compete regularly. It's important for team members to attend all practices. That way the team improves and learns to play together. This keeps team members motivated to attend. Nita's friend Lidia might feel tired or want to do something else during practice. However, her commitment to her team motivates her to attend practices.

Avoiding Boredom

Some people get bored working out. Keeping a log turns one person into a team. Through a log, one person acts as coach, team member, and record keeper. The person tracks his or her progress and sets goals. It's a good idea to make a fitness log special. Some people may buy a cool journal. Others may decorate a notebook by pasting pictures of people who inspire them on it. This encourages people to write in their log.

Another boredom buster is working out with a friend. A friend counts on you to show up. The two people working out provide each other with company and motivation.

"Hey, Kyle. I got us a new tape to listen to while we

KYLE AND GRADY, AGE 17

work out. It's by that band we saw on TV last week."

"Cool. Can I keep it if I do 100 push-ups?" Grady asked.

"Sure. But if I do 101, I keep it."

Conquering the Enemy Without: External Obstacles

An external obstacle is anything outside a person's control. One external obstacle to fitness might be a lack of opportunities in the community. Some schools or local community centers may not offer sports programs. Fitness centers may be too expensive or far away. These obstacles do not need to keep people from getting fit. There are dozens of other options. Chapter 6 can help you choose a program that fits your needs.

Another obstacle could be the people in a person's life. A fitness program takes time from a person's day. It may leave a little less time to spend with friends, family, or a girlfriend or boyfriend. At first these people may object to the change in schedule. They likely will understand if given an explanation. Working out reduces stress. That means people who work out may be more relaxed than people who do not. As a result, people who work out may have fewer stressful encounters with the people in their life.

Points to Consider

What do you think are some of the main reasons people do not exercise?

What are some things that could motivate people to exercise?

What in a person's environment might prevent him or her from getting fit?

What advice would you give to people who say they want to work out but don't have the time?

Chapter Overview

The first step to starting a fitness program is asking yourself why you want to be fit.

Another important step is to set long-term, short-term, immediate, and back-up goals.

A workout journal can help a person stay on track.

A poster with goals listed on it can help keep a person motivated.

It usually takes about three to four months to notice the benefits of exercise.

Chapter **3**

Steps to Success

Why Do You Want to Be Fit?

The first step in starting a fitness program is asking yourself why you want to get fit. Do you want to look better? Maybe you want to feel better. Do you want to have more strength and endurance? Perhaps you want to try out for a sport. Whatever your reason, it is important to make sure the reason is yours. For example, some teens may get fit just to please parents or someone they have a crush on. Teens should get fit for themselves.

Goals

Another important step is to set goals. The four different types of goals are long-term, short-term, immediate, and back-up goals.

Long-Term Goals

Long-term goals focus on the big picture. These are goals you hope to accomplish in three to six months. These long-term goals should be realistic. For example, Ernesto wants to complete a 5-kilometer race that is 4 months away. Marcy's goal is to make a sports team next season. Shanelle wants to look fit and trim in her new bathing suit.

Short-Term Goals

Short-term goals help you get through your daily workout. These goals allow you to feel successful during each workout. Here are some examples of short-term goals:

Run one mile today without stopping.

Improve on last week's bench press.

Ride a bike for 45 minutes instead of 30 minutes.

Immediate Goals

Immediate goals can help you to get through a difficult workout. Sometimes it may feel like you cannot make it through a workout another minute. At times like these, it helps to create some immediate goals.

Myth: People who do not achieve the goals they set are losers.

Fact: If people give it their all and don't meet their goal, chances are the goal they set was too hard.

For example, if you're riding a stationary bike, you could lower the difficulty level from six to three. You could allow yourself to stay at half effort for two minutes. Then for one minute, you would really pedal hard. If you repeated this cycle 10 times, the 30 minutes would be up.

Vijay felt like his workout was lasting forever. He thought of a trick that a friend had taught him. Vijay imagined that he was running against a great athlete. If he finished his mile in the next nine minutes, he won. Vijay finished the mile in less than nine minutes.

VIJAY, AGE 18

Back-up Goals

Setting back-up goals can help a person to avoid feelings of failure. If you don't achieve your ultimate goal, you won't give up altogether. For example, your main goal may be to run a 5K nonstop. Your secondary goal may be to simply finish the race, even if it means walking.

A workout journal can help a person learn about his or her personal exercise patterns. After a month, a person might say, "Hmm, I can never seem to get a Friday workout in. Maybe that's expecting too much of myself."

Keep a Workout Journal

A workout journal keeps a person honest and on track. At the end of the week or month, people can look back and be proud of their progress. This often inspires people to do more. Such a log can help determine whether goals are realistic. People do not have to wonder what is working. The log provides an account.

A workout journal includes fitness-test results and long-term, short-term, immediate, and back-up goals. It also should contain the date, time, and length of the workout, what was done, and how it felt.

It is important to track your improvements against your own efforts from the week or month before. You should avoid comparing yourself to an outside standard such as how high a professional basketball player can jump.

Maria loved Daisy Fuentes, who was a great volleyball player

MARIA, AGE 14

and a beautiful TV star. Maria took a magazine picture of Daisy and pasted it to some poster board. She drew the words "Work it, Maria," coming from Daisy's mouth. At the bottom of the poster, Maria wrote her goals in big, colorful letters.

Make a Goal Poster

Some people find goal posters helpful. These are made by writing goals on a large sheet of paper. A person makes it special by pasting or drawing inspirational images on it. The poster should be put where it will be seen every day. It is important to include a reward on the goal sheet. The reward might be a new CD or pair of jeans. Other rewards could be an evening with friends or a good book.

Stick With It

Exercise may be hard for people to stick with until they see and feel results. However, once many people reach that point, they work out because they want to, not because they have to. As a rule, most people need to work out regularly for three to four months to fully appreciate exercise. Like other aspects of daily life, fitness takes planning. People who want to be fit have to make exercise a part of their daily routine.

Points to Consider

What might be a long-term fitness goal for you? Why do you want to achieve it?

What type of goal do you think is most important? Explain.

What do you think is the biggest advantage to keeping a workout journal?

Chapter Overview

The five kinds of fitness are aerobic endurance, muscular strength, muscular endurance, flexibility, and body composition.

Aerobic endurance is the ability to use the body's major muscle groups over time at a moderate intensity.

Examples of muscular strength activities are using the muscles to push or pull something and sprinting. Muscular strength activities use anaerobic energy.

The ability to repeatedly move heavy objects is muscular endurance.

Flexibility is the ability to stretch muscles, ligaments, and tendons. It is the range of motion at a joint.

Body composition is the percentages of fat, bone, and muscle in the body.

Chapter **4**

Five Kinds of Fitness

In general, there are five kinds of fitness—aerobic endurance, muscular strength, muscular endurance, flexibility, and body composition. Deciding which of these is most important can help a person select the right fitness program.

Aerobic Endurance

Aerobic endurance involves the ability to use the body's large muscle groups. In aerobic endurance, these muscle groups are used at moderate intensity over long periods of time. Jogging, in-line skating, and swimming are examples of aerobic exercise. The aerobic system uses oxygen to break down carbohydrates and convert them into energy. Aerobic workouts are ideal for strengthening the heart and lowering body fat.

Aerobic endurance can be achieved by maintaining moderately intense activity for periods of at least 15 to 30 minutes. Workouts should take place three to four times a week. In the beginning, workout time should be increased slowly. For example, a person might add two to five minutes more a session until achieving his or her goal. Generally, the more aerobic demands made on the body, the more fit it gets.

Jessica saw Maya lying on the weight bench. Maya **JESSICA AND MAYA, AGE 17** was getting ready to lift the weights. Jessica offered to spot Maya during the bench press, "Hey, Maya. I'll count for you."

Jessica helped Maya count and encouraged her. "Wow, you've really gotten stronger these past few months."

Muscular Strength

Maya's bench pressing is an example of muscular strength. Her muscles generated extreme amounts of force in a short period of time. Muscular strength activities build muscle. They also increase the body's connective tissue size and density. They do this by enlarging cells or "building" muscles. Having stronger muscles and connective tissues make injury less likely. Strength exercises can improve the way the body looks.

To build muscular strength it's a good idea to stagger exercises. Spend one workout on the upper body and the next on the lower body. Concentrate on activities that work specific muscle groups. Work slowly and concentrate on form.

Using muscular strength requires anaerobic activity. During anaerobic activity such as sprinting, the body uses carbohydrates for energy. This anaerobic energy is produced in short-term bursts. Therefore, anaerobic activity only can be sustained for a few minutes. Then the body needs a short recovery rest.

Muscular Endurance

Muscular endurance is the ability to move heavy objects again and again using the muscles. The length of time a person can keep up the activity is a factor of muscular endurance. One example of muscular endurance is doing push-ups. Every fitness activity requires muscular endurance. Repeatedly lifting a weight requires it. Intense aerobic activities such as biking also require it.

Just like aerobic endurance and muscular strength, muscular endurance is increased by slight overexertion. That means a person works slightly beyond his or her limit. When lifting weights, a person should average 3 sets of 12 to 20 repetitions, or reps. A repetition is one complete motion of an exercise. A set is a group of repetitions done one after the other. Doing sets of repetitions is an excellent way to build endurance. However, a person should not overdo it. It is important to increase efforts only slightly each time to avoid injury.

RACHEL, AGE 13

Rachel sat on the floor with her legs stretched out in front of her. She slid her hands along the floor toward her toes. She smiled. She was able to stretch a little farther than she could a month earlier. Rachel wanted to improve her flexibility for dance class. Her mother had promised Rachel lessons.

Flexibility

Flexibility is the ability to stretch muscles and the tendons and ligaments that connect them to the bones. Stretching these tough bands of tissue beyond their usual limits increases flexibility. Each stretch is maintained for 10 to 60 seconds. The tissues eventually adjust to these new limits.

Increased flexibility decreases the risk of injury during exercise. It also improves exercise performance. Some activities such as yoga and gymnastics require more flexibility than other activities do. Yoga is a system of exercises for well-being.

Muscle tissue burns more calories than fat does, even while a person is resting.

Any fitness activity should include some stretching. Stretching is done after warming up but before a workout. Warmed-up muscles are more limber, and less at risk for tears or pulls. Stretching should never be painful. People should stretch only until they feel a slight tug of the muscle, not pain. For maximum results, a person should stretch several times a day at least five times a week. A person does not have to work out every time he or she stretches.

Stretching after a workout helps vigorously exercised muscles by relaxing them. It also prevents cramping. Stretching exercises can be found in chapter 7.

Body Composition

Body composition describes the percentages of fat, bone, and muscle in the body. These percentages may provide an overall view of a person's health and fitness.

The word *fat* often is associated with weight. However, it shouldn't be. Many people who are physically fit weigh more than what a health chart might suggest. This is because these physically fit people have gained muscle, and muscle weighs more than fat. A person who is overweight is not necessarily obese, or extremely fat. Having too much body fat poses health risks such as heart disease, high blood pressure, and diabetes.

MYTH VS. FACT

Myth: No pain, no gain.

Fact: Actually, pain is the body's way of telling a person that there is something wrong.

The amount of healthy body fat differs for men and women. A healthy male's body should be approximately 12 to 18 percent fat. The percentage for females is slightly higher. Approximately 14 to 23 percent of their body composition should be fat. A person should avoid having too little body fat. A reasonable amount of body fat has benefits. Fat helps store energy and maintain body temperature.

It is hard to determine someone's body composition accurately. Measures such as water displacement or skin-fold measurement can give fairly accurate estimations. Water displacement measurement involves being weighed under water with special equipment. Skin-fold measurement is a technique that uses a special device to measure the fat underneath the skin. Often, doctors offer body composition tests. The athletic trainer at your school may be able to perform the test. Someone at a local fitness center may be able to do the test as well.

Moderation and Patience Are Key

In all of your fitness pursuits, don't overdo it. Don't expect to achieve your ultimate goal in a day. Working out too hard too quickly could result in injury. Anaerobic activity produces a substance called lactic acid that builds up in muscle tissue. This buildup can be temporarily painful. By stretching after a workout, you can reduce the chance of this happening.

The body needs time to recover and gain strength. Therefore, rest is important. Alternate workout days and stagger the intensity of workouts. This can aid in overall improvement and prevent injury.

Points to Consider

What is muscular strength? What activities do you do that require muscular strength?

Why is stretching important?

Do you think today's American culture encourages people to have too little body fat? Explain.

Why could having too little body fat be a problem?

Chapter
Overview

It's a good idea to find out how fit you are before starting a fitness program.

Assessment tests can measure your current level of fitness.

It is important to write down the results and the date of your fitness tests.

Some tests you can do yourself. These tests measure your heart rate, aerobic fitness, muscular strength, and flexibility.

Some tests can help estimate how much of your body is fat. A doctor or trainer can probably give you one of these tests.

Chapter **5**

How Fit Are You?

Griffin was tired of being skinny. He wanted to build muscle. He wanted to be able to do 100 push-ups when his coach yelled, "Drop and give me 20!"

GRIFFIN, AGE 18

Griffin had a plan to improve his muscular strength and endurance. He needed to do one thing first, though. He needed to see how fit he already was. He needed to do a self-assessment.

Before beginning any fitness plan, it's important to record how fit you currently are. This means doing a few short tests. These are not the kinds of tests you can flunk. They just give you your starting point. These assessment tests determine your heart rate, strength, flexibility, and body fat. The information from these tests can help you set goals. As you progress, you can look back at these figures. They will show you how far you have come.

Heart Rate

Heart rate also is known as pulse. It is the number of times a person's heart beats in one minute. Heart rate should first be measured while resting. An ideal heart rate is between 60 and 90 beats per minute. Usually after a month or two of regular exercise, a person's resting heart rate lowers. This means that the heart has become more efficient. In the long run, a lower heart rate saves the heart from doing extra work.

Myth: Fitness is determined by how many miles you can run or how many pounds you can lift.

Fact: Fitness is achieved when all the body's systems are in good working order.

GRIFFIN'S HEART RATE

Griffin took his resting heart rate. It was 65. Pretty good, he thought. Last month it was at 70. Maybe next month it would be 60.

The easiest place to take your own pulse is on your wrist. The following chart shows how to do it.

Resting Heart Rate Test

For this test you need a watch or clock with a second hand.

Rest the ring, middle, and index fingers of one hand lightly on the opposite wrist.

Place fingers directly between the base of the hand and the thumb.

Feel for a beat.

Count the beats for a full minute.

The number of beats counted is your pulse. Another way to take your pulse is to count your heartbeats for 15 seconds and multiply by 4.

Tips for aerobic workouts:

Be intensely active for 30 minutes.

Work out three to four times a week.

Increase the workout time slowly until your goal is achieved.

A great aerobic workout is dancing for 45 minutes or stair climbing for 25 minutes.

How Fit Is Your Heart?

The heart's rate while a person is working his or her heart measures aerobic fitness. The fastest the heart rate should be is about 220 beats a minute minus a person's age. This number is a person's maximum heart rate. During exercise, a person should maintain his or her target heart rate zone. This rate should be 60 to 85 percent of the person's maximum heart rate.

The first chart tells how to determine your target heart rate. The second chart explains how to test your aerobic fitness.

Determining Your Target Heart Rate

Subtract your age from 220.

Multiply that number by .75 (75%).

The number you get is what your heart rate should be when you work out.

For example, Rich is 16. He subtracts 16 from 220 and multiplies by .75. That equals 153. When he works out, his heart rate should be 153 beats per minute.

Aerobic Fitness Test

For this test you need a watch with a second hand, a pencil, and paper. You also need a treadmill or an outdoor running track.

Warm up by walking slowly for 5 to 10 minutes.

After you warm up, write down the exact time.

Walk a mile as quickly as you can.

Right before you stop, take your pulse. Write down the number.

Write down the exact time you stop. Subtract the first time from the second. The result is the number of minutes it took to finish the mile.

One minute after completing the mile, take your pulse again. Write down the number. This is your recovery pulse. Your recovery pulse should be much lower than your pulse taken right after completing the mile.

Keep the numbers in a safe place. Try this test again in a few months. Your mile should get faster as you become more fit. Your first pulse measure should drop. Also, there should be a greater difference between your first pulse and your recovery pulse.

How Strong Are Your Muscles?

Muscle strength is something else important to measure. Two major areas to test are upper- and middle-body strength. It's easy to test your upper-body strength. Count the number of push-ups you can do without stopping. A crunch test is a good way to measure middle-body strength. Here's one way to do it.

Middle-Body Strength Test—The Crunch

Lie flat on your back on the floor with your knees bent.

Slide your feet under something that won't move. (A couch works well.)

Place your arms at your sides. Your hands should be on the floor.

Curl your head, neck, and shoulder blades upward.

Slide your hands forward along the floor about 2 inches. You should feel your stomach muscles tense.

Return your head, neck, and shoulder blades to the floor.

Repeat until you are too tired to use the correct form.

Write down the number of crunches you can do.

Strong muscles help protect a person during exercise. They support joints and can help prevent injuries.

How Flexible Are You?

Chung could bench press his own weight. He could do 100 push-ups without stopping. But Chung could not touch his toes without bending his knees. He knew that he'd have to be more flexible to consider himself truly fit.

CHUNG, AGE 18

One way to test your flexibility is the sit-and-reach test. The following chart explains how the test works.

Flexibility Test—Sit-and-Reach

Tape a yardstick to the floor at the 15-inch mark.

Sit on the floor facing the yardstick. The zero mark should be closest to you. Your feet should be about 10 inches apart and your toes should point forward.

Place your heels at the 15-inch mark.

Reach your hands out toward the yardstick.

Slide your fingers along the yardstick as far as possible.

Your score is the highest number you reach, to the nearest inch.

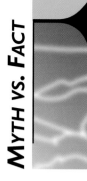
Myth: Women who lift weights develop big, bulky muscles.

Fact: Big muscles are the result of male hormones. Women don't have enough of these hormones naturally to make their muscles huge.

What Is Your Body Fat?

Weight can be misleading. Two people who are the same weight and height may have very different bodies. They could have different size bone frames. They could have different amounts of muscle. They might also differ in amounts of body fat.

Excess body fat can be a fitness concern. It's helpful to know how much of your body is fat and how much is lean body tissue. A doctor or a trainer at a fitness center can probably test your body fat percentage.

How to Use the Tests

The tests suggested in this chapter can give you a general sense of your fitness level. Having a high score right now is not important. What is important is how much you improve each time you retake the tests. For example, a person may first be able to do only 10 push-ups without stopping. This isn't good or bad. Several weeks later the person tests again. This time the person does 16 push-ups without stopping. Any improvement is something a person can be proud of.

The Next Step

Now you're ready to choose a fitness activity. Remember, it is important to choose activities that are fun for you. Fitness goals can be reached in many different and exciting ways. The next chapter provides some ideas.

Points to Consider

Why do you think it is important to know your resting heart rate?

Which of the tests in this chapter might you do and why?

Some people may not have tried these tests. Do you think these people have a good idea of their fitness level? Explain.

Why is it important to write down the results of these fitness tests?

Chapter Overview

You should choose a fitness focus that is important to you. However, any workout program should include some exercise related to all five kinds of fitness.

Working out alone is one way to exercise. Some possibilities include jumping rope, following exercise videos, running, walking, and joining a gym.

Another exercise option is working out with a friend. A friend can help keep you motivated.

Joining a sports team is another good way to get exercise. Being with friends and the desire to win may help motivate you.

Clubs and classes provide the fun of exercising with other people around, but often without the competition of teams.

Chapter **6**

Finding Fitness

You now know some details about your fitness level. You also know your goals. The next step is to consider what activities can help you reach your goals.

After watching the Olympics, Ruben knew he wanted to excel as a swimmer. He had good form, but he wasn't fast enough. What he needed was more endurance and strength. He needed to build muscle as well as heart and lung power.

RUBEN, AGE 14

Choosing Your Fitness Focus

The following questions can help you decide on a fitness focus:

Do you want to run, bike, and swim like a world-class triathlete? Then your goal is aerobic fitness.

Do you want to lift a 75-pound canoe and carry it around a dam? If so, your fitness goals are muscular strength and endurance.

Do you want to bend and stretch like a gymnast? Then your goal is flexibility.

Do you hope to be lean? Then your fitness goals are fat loss and muscle tone.

Do you desire all of the above qualities? Then you should plan a workout that has aerobic, flexibility, and strength-building components, or parts.

Deciding which fitness goals are most important to you helps to narrow down your workout choices. Any fitness plan, however, should include at least some of each fitness component.

A second-hand sporting equipment store can help keep workout costs down. However, it is important to be careful when buying shoes. Shoes are specifically designed to take the impact of a workout instead of the body. Used shoes may not protect you from injuries.

Sweating Solo

After choosing a fitness focus, ask yourself if you want to exercise alone or with others. Some teens prefer to exercise alone. They see it as a good time to think and to release stress. Exercising alone has one important advantage. You can work out when and where you want to.

Many activities are available for people who want to work out alone. If you like to be outside, running, biking, brisk walking, skiing, or skating may be for you. If you live near a park, check to see if they rent skates or skis. If you like the activity enough, you may want to buy equipment from a used sporting goods store.

Home is a good workout place for some people. It is convenient and you can use your own shower. Your family may even own some fitness equipment. However, expensive equipment isn't necessary to get a good workout. A simple jump rope works great. Jump ropes are cheap and easy to use. Just turn on some music and jump to it for 10 minutes. Jog in place for 10 minutes. Throw in 3 sets of 15 push-ups, crunches, and leg squats, or bends. This makes a well-rounded workout.

Fitness videos can help with goals to build muscle and increase endurance and flexibility. Videos exist for almost any fitness interest, from kickboxing to tai chi. Tai chi is an ancient physical art form that involves stretching, breathing, and circular motion. Video stores have fitness videos for rent. Most public libraries have them available.

Another option is to join a gym. A community gym can be a good place to start. Most have the means to help a person achieve all five kinds of fitness. Gyms usually have machines for cardiovascular, or heart and blood vessel, health. These machines include stationary bikes, stairclimbers, and treadmills. It is important to ask a staff person how to use the machines before starting. Gyms also have weight-lifting equipment. Again, have someone who works there demonstrate how to use the weights. Some gyms offer different types of classes. These classes will be discussed later in the chapter.

Sweating With a Friend

You may find it's more fun to have someone to encourage and support you while you work out. A friend or family member may be a good partner. Chances are, your workout partner will become a better friend. Also, setting a time to work out with someone else means you're less likely to skip a workout.

Chad waited at the running track

for Leon. He and Leon met at 5:00 every afternoon to jog five miles. It was 5:15. Where in the heck was Leon?

Chad went to a nearby pay phone to call Leon. "Hey, it's 5:15. Where are you? Do you want to be in shape for the start of the football season or not?"

Exercise with friends doesn't have to be a workout session. Riding bikes, hiking, swimming, and in-line skating are all great ways to get exercise.

Team Sweat

Another way to work out with others is to join a team. Many schools have sports teams. Community centers or local parks may have team sports as well. Team sports have their advantages. One advantage is that a coach can teach you what to do. He or she can keep track of your progress. The desire to win may really motivate you, too.

Foot tennis is played in Malaysia, usually between two teams of two players. A net is stretched across the middle of a playing area. Players try to pass a ball back and forth over the net using only their feet, knees, and thighs. Each time the ball drops, the other team gets a point.

Octopush is an underwater hockey game played on the floor of a swimming pool. This game started in South Africa in the 1960s. The players wear skin-diving equipment and use miniature hockey sticks and a hockey puck. The players follow the rules of ice hockey.

The team sports available differ from community to community. Talking with the athletic director at your school or community center can help you find out what sports are offered. The director also might know which sport would be right for you.

There are a variety of sports to try. Some can be played indoors. Some can be played outdoors. A few can be played either inside or outside. Some ideas are hockey, basketball, volleyball, wrestling, gymnastics, dance, swimming, rowing, or martial, or self-defense, arts. A few other popular sports are rugby/football, water polo, baseball/softball, soccer, field hockey, and lacrosse. Tennis and track also are popular sports.

JANELLE, AGE 17

In phys ed class, Janelle always came in last when the kids ran. In basketball, she tripped over her own feet. Janelle wanted to be more fit. But she wondered how. She hated the idea of team sports, and she knew she'd never exercise alone. She thought it was just too boring. Then she remembered an ad she had seen for a karate class. Janelle thought that maybe she should sign up.

Classes and Clubs

Some people such as Janelle don't like team sports or exercising alone. For these people, clubs and classes are another option. Clubs and classes are somewhere in between working out alone and with a team. They allow you to be with other people, but the instructor is the focus. Participants can blend into the group or get social. It's their decision.

Class and club activities usually involve groups of people. However, they are not necessarily competitive. Popular classes include karate and other martial arts as well as rock climbing, aerobics classes, and yoga.

Points to Consider

Which fitness focus would you choose? Why?

What are some of the advantages of exercising alone? What are some of the disadvantages?

What would you say to someone who said, "I'd work out but health clubs are too expensive"?

What are some clubs or classes available at your school and in your community?

Chapter Overview

A complete workout has four parts—warming up, stretching, working out, and cooling down.

Eating the right foods in the right amounts is essential for fitness.

The body needs plenty of water to work its best.

A varied routine of exercise is the key to total fitness.

Chapter **7**

Go For It!

Elise warmed up for her workout by jogging in place for three minutes. Then she did a few stretches. Next she did a jump rope routine for 10 minutes. To cool down, Elise walked in place for five minutes. She finished up with some more stretches. Her whole workout took less than 30 minutes.

ELISE, AGE 16

The Four-Part Workout

Elise's workout included four parts—warming up, stretching, working out, and cooling down. Successful workouts include all four of these components.

1. Warming Up

Warming up is essential in any fitness activity. It helps the body move blood to the working muscles and helps prevent injury. What if you join a team and they don't warm up? Then it is a good idea to talk with the coach about warming up. The following is a good warm-up activity:

Do an easy jog for three minutes.

Reach your arms up and down 10 times.

Lean to one side as you reach up one arm. Alternate with the other side. Do this 10 times.

2. Stretching

A warm-up readies the body for stretching, another essential part of any fitness activity. Stretching keeps joints working within a normal range of motion. Here are three stretches to try:

The straddle

Sit with your legs wide apart. Extend one leg. Bend the opposite knee.

Keep your back straight. Lean forward slowly and grasp the toes of the extended leg.

Then switch which leg is extended and which one is bent. Repeat the stretch.

Butterfly stretch

Sit on the floor with the sole of your shoes together.

Use your elbows to gently press your knees toward the floor.

Lean forward and count to 10.

Shoulder stretch

Stand with your right side next to a wall. Bend your arm at the elbow. Place the palm of your right hand against the wall. Fingers should point up toward the ceiling.

Turn your torso, or the part of your body between the neck and the waist, away from the hand. Turn only until you feel a stretch across the chest and shoulder.

Repeat on the left side.

3. Working Out

The main part of a workout includes endurance and aerobic activities. These exercises should be done at least 15 to 30 minutes, 3 times a week. Some examples of endurance and aerobic activities are:

Jogging

Aerobic dancing

Bicycling (10 to 13 miles per hour)

Hip-hop dancing

Swimming (30 yards per minute)

Myth: Regular food is okay for building strength, but supplements and sports foods and drinks are best.

Fact: These products aren't necessary. They are expensive, too. A teen's body cannot tell the difference between protein that comes from a product or from food. The protein contained in most supplements is approximately equal to that in one cup of milk or one serving of meat.

4. Cooling Down

The body needs to cool down after a workout. A person should avoid lying down or standing still immediately after exercising. Otherwise, blood can collect in the legs. This can cause dizziness or fainting. It can cause nausea, or make a person feel like he or she is going to throw up. A cool-down returns the body to a relaxed state. One good idea is to walk around for 5 or 10 minutes. After the walk, mild exercise or stretching is a good idea.

Food and Fitness

Eating the right food is another necessity for fitness. Combining healthy food with exercise can help people to reach their fitness potential.

An excellent guide to healthy eating is the Food Guide Pyramid. The foods in the pyramid include the nutrients that the body needs to work well. The pyramid suggests the right combination of vitamins, minerals, proteins, carbohydrates, and other nutrients to eat. It recommends eating certain amounts from each food group. This food combination gives people the nutrients they need to get the most out of a workout.

MARTIN, AGE 15

"Only pasta tonight, Mom, no veggies. I'm loading up on carbohydrates. We've got a big meet tomorrow," Martin said.

"Why carbohydrates?" Martin's mom asked.

"Energy."

"Where'd you hear that?"

"It's just common knowledge, Mom. Pasta's full of carbos that supply energy."

Some teens like Martin have heard about adults eating only pasta before a big athletic event. However, this does not work well for a teen. A teen's body needs different foods to perform its best. Eating from only one food group probably will let a teen down.

Eating enough food is important. Athletes should not limit the food they eat unless instructed by a doctor. Most active teens need all the calories they normally consume to give them power and strength. Cutting calories can limit performance.

In addition, teen growth spurts require some extra body fat. This means a need for extra calories. Some teens may have a coach, friend, or trainer who suggests the teen go on a diet. The teen should not do anything until talking with his or her doctor. The doctor can decide if a diet is necessary. He or she can work with the teen to come up with a healthy eating and exercise program.

Water

Food isn't the only key to unleashing the body's power. Water is just as important. It's needed to keep the body working at its peak. The body needs to be hydrated, or have water to function, during exercise.

During strenuous exercise, the body loses water through sweat. The body can lose large amounts of water this way. When exercising, it is easy to become overheated. This can limit performance. It can be dangerous in hot or humid weather. Therefore, it is important to stay properly hydrated during exercise. Drinking fluid before, during, and after exercise, a game, or athletic event is the best way to stay hydrated. Here are the recommended amounts of water to drink:

10 to 12 ounces—1 or 2 hours before activity

10 ounces—10 to 15 minutes before activity

3 to 4 ounces—every 15 minutes during activity

About 16 ounces for every pound lost through sweat (for teens this equals a cup or two)—right after activity

To avoid boredom, a person should do a variety of fitness activities. For example, someone might bike one day and play soccer the next.

There is nothing wrong with drinking more than the amounts listed if a person is still thirsty. Likewise, a teen should drink whether or not he or she is thirsty. Thirst is a signal that the body has needed liquids for quite some time. Water is the best choice to satisfy thirst. The body absorbs it more easily than any other liquid.

Variety Is Key

A varied exercise routine is the final key to fitness. Blake's schedule for the week shows a good example of variety.

BLAKE, AGE 16

Monday: Karate class

Tuesday: Relax

Wednesday: Warm up and stretch; jog three miles

Thursday: Relax

Friday: Play one-on-one with Paul

Saturday: Rake and mow lawn

Sunday: Mountain bike with Kurt and T.J.

Calorie burners:

Activity	Calories burned per hour	Activity	Calories burned per hour
Housework	150 to 250	Brisk swimming	360 to 500
Raking leaves	225	Basketball	360 to 660
Lawn mowing	250	Bowling	400
Brisk walking on a level surface	360	Biking (10 mph)	420
		Downhill skiing	500 to 600
		Jogging	600 to 750

A varied exercise routine should include some kind of activity five times a week. The goal is 30 minutes of activity 5 days a week. Three of these days should include vigorous exercise. These three days should be spread out through the week. The week can be rounded out with other kinds of activity. This could include biking or walking to school or the mall instead of taking the car or bus. Mowing the lawn, raking the yard, and shoveling snow are other exercise ideas.

The body builds fitness over time. To keep the body fit, it is important to make exercise a part of your weekly routine.

Points to Consider

What are the four parts of a workout?

Do you think it is okay to skip one part of a workout? Why or why not?

How does your diet compare with what the Food Guide Pyramid suggests? How could you improve your fitness level through your diet?

Have you watched people work out or practice for sports? Do they seem well hydrated? Explain.

Why do you think it's important to get different kinds of exercise?

Glossary

aerobic (air-OH-bik)—requiring oxygen, or air

anaerobic (AN-air-oh-bik)—not requiring oxygen, or air

carbohydrate (kar-boh-HYE-drate)—a substance in food such as bread, rice, and potatoes that provides energy

cardiovascular (kar-dee-oh-VASS-kyuh-lur)—relating to the heart and blood vessels

dehydrate (dee-HYE-drate)—to lose water or body fluids

endorphin (en-DOR-fin)—a substance created by the brain that reduces pain

endurance (en-DUR-uhnss)—the ability to continue through a physically stressful activity

fitness (FIT-ness)—when a person's body is in good physical shape; a person's heart, lungs, muscles, and blood vessels are in good working order.

hydrate (HYE-drate)—to give water

ligament (LIG-uh-muhnt)—a band of tough, fibrous tissue that connects bones or holds an organ in place

motivation (moh-tuh-VAY-shun)—the encouragement or desire to do something

obstacle (OB-stuh-kuhl)—something that gets in the way

self-esteem (self-ess-TEEM)—a feeling of pride and respect for yourself

stamina (STAM-uh-nuh)—the energy and strength to keep doing something for a long time

tendon (TEN-duhn)—a strong, thick cord or band of tissue that joins a muscle to a bone or other body part

For More Information

Bull, Deborah C., and Torje Eike. *Totally Fit.* New York: DK Publishing, 1998.

Gebhardt, Kris. *Training the Teenager for the Game of Their Life.* Indianapolis, IN: Sideline Sports, 1998.

Reef, Catherine. *Stay Fit: Build a Strong Body.* New York: Twenty-First Century Books, 1993.

Schlosberg, Suzanne, and Liz Neporent. *Fitness for Dummies.* Foster City, CA: IDG Books, 1996.

Schwager, Tina, and Michele Schuerger. *The Right Moves: A Girl's Guide to Getting Fit and Feeling Good.* Minneapolis, MN: Free Spirit, 1998.

Useful Addresses and Internet Sites

American Council on Exercise
5820 Oberlin Drive, Suite 102
San Diego, CA 92121
1-800-529-8227
www.acefitness.org

American Heart Association
National Center
7272 Greenville Avenue
Dallas, TX 75231
1-800-242-8721
www.americanheart.org

Health Canada
Childhood and Youth Division
9th Floor Jeanne Mance Building
Tunney's Pasture, Mail Stop 1909C2
Ottawa, ON K1A 0K9
CANADA

President's Council on Physical Fitness and
Sports
Suite 738-H
200 Independence Avenue Southwest
Washington, DC 20201

Shape Up America!
6707 Democracy Boulevard
Suite 306
Bethesda, MD 20817
www.shapeup.org

Canadian Association for the Advancement of
Women and Sport and Physical Activity
www.caaws.ca
Encourages girls and women to participate in
sports

Exercise For Your Health
ext.msstate.edu/pubs/pub1993.htm
Gives teens information on flexibility, strength,
and endurance and provides exercise examples

The Fitness Files
fyiowa.webpoint.com/fitness/index.htm
Provides information on a variety of fitness
topics

FitTeen.com
www.fitteen.com
Offers a glossary of fitness terms, a teen-
fitness chat room, workout charts, and sample
routines

KidsHealth.org
www.kidshealth.org
Provides teens with information on food and
fitness and growing up healthy

Index

Index continued